I AM DOUG the PUG®

Published by Scholastic Inc., *Publishers since 1920*. SCHOLASTIC and associated logos are trademarks and/or registered trademarks of Scholastic Inc.

ISBN 978-1-338-35953-4

10 9 8 7 6 5 4 3 2   19 20 21 22 23

Printed in the U.S.A.   40
First printing 2019

Illustrations by Mercedes Padró
Book design by Mercedes Padró and Becky James
Written by Megan Faulkner

I AM DOUG the PUG®

WHAT'S INSIDE?

Meet Doug.. 9

A Pug for All Seasons!..18

Help Doug Get Red Carpet Ready............................... 23

Activity: Rate Doug's Costumes 32

Doug's Style Advice.. 38

Doug's Rules for Life.. 44

Activity: What Would Doug Say?................................48

Activity: Happy Holipugs Word Search.......................52

Doug's Selfie Tips...55

Activity: Caption Match... 62

Quiz: What Would Doug Do?....................................65

Doug & Friends... 72

Activity: Where in the World is Doug? 75

Quiz: How Well Do You Know Doug?...........................80

Doug's Recipe for Success...................................... 82

Answer Key... 86

Dress Doug!... 90

MEET DOUG

Hi! I'm Doug.

I'm a pizza-loving, red-carpet-walking, jet-setting, world-famous pug living my best life. I'm here to share my tips, rules, advice, and recipe for success so you can live your best life, too! Along the way there's some fun activities to do — and of course, lots of pictures of me!

9

ALL ABOUT ME

NICE TO MEET U

DO I LOOK MAJESTIC?

Name: Doug the Pug

Known as:
The King of Pop Culture

MUSIC CITY, USA, USA, USA!

Hometown:
Nashville, Tennessee

BUT I CELEBRATE EVERY DAY

Birthday: May 20, 2012

Family: Leslie (human), Rob (human), and Fiona (cat)

STOP TOUCHING ME, FIONA!

MY ONE TRUE LOVE

1 FOR U AND 5 FOR ME

Favorite Food: Pizza

Favorite Dessert: Donuts

IF ONLY I COULD READ

Favorite Drink: Coffee

LEAVES
ARE FOR
ROLLING IN

Favorite Season: Fall

PRETTIEST
PUGKIN IN
THE PATCH

Favorite Holiday: Pugoween

Favorite Activities

Relaxing at home

HOLD MY CALLS

Dressing up

I CLEAN UP NICELY

Traveling

OFF TO EXPLORE THE WORLD

Making new friends

NO SUCH THING AS TOO MANY FRIENDS!

14

Taking selfies

Staying Social

Insta-pug since 2015

Tweeting isn't just for
birds anymore

It's **DOUG** the **PUG** in

A PUG FOR ALL SEASONS

FALL

WINTER

PUG FOR ALL
★ SEASONS ★
MOVIE NIGHT | ROW 05 | SEAT 23
TONIGHT!

SPRING

SUMMER

21

HELP DOUG

GET RED CARPET READY

What's it like being a world-famous pug? Spend the day with me and find out!

Stretching helps me wake up!

I call this pose Downward Doug!

Sometimes I get *too* relaxed . . .

Maybe this coffee will perk me up?

Breakfast of champions!

I have a big event tonight. What should I wear? A costume?

I'M A LOVER NOT A BITER!

Everyone loves a pugicorn!

SAVING THIS FOR THE OSCARS!

STOP COPYING ME, FIONA!

27

RATE DOUG'S COSTUMES

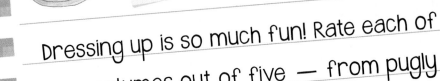

Dressing up is so much fun! Rate each of my costumes out of five — from pugly to *pugmazing* — by circling or coloring in the paw prints.

PUGLY	🐾
PUGERRIFIC	🐾🐾
PUGALICIOUS	🐾🐾🐾
PUGTASTIC	🐾🐾🐾🐾
PUGMAZING!	🐾🐾🐾🐾🐾

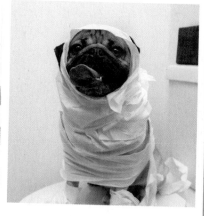

Cutest mummy ever?

I vant to eat ur pizza

Puggington Bear

Pugacado

Pugachu

P.U.G. phone home

But I'm too cute to
be the beast

Adorable, I am

Winnie the Pug

U can never have
too much bacon

34

Ready for Pugwarts!

Princess Fiona & Shrek

3 heads r better
than 1

Mary had a little pug

Rollin' with my gnomie

Here comes the pug

It's the cirrrrcle of life

Am I even a tiny bit scary?

36

I'm a sweet treat

Two peas on a pug

I cast a spell on u

The Dark Pug Rises

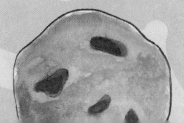

DOUG'S STYLE ADVICE

Clothes are a great way to show your personality. Here's how I show mine!

Have a robe for EVERY MOOD!

Put a **TOWEL** on it

TOO TALL

TOO TIGHT

JUST RIGHT

41

SHADES take your look to the next level

A beanie a day keeps the BAD HAIR AWAY

Monday

Tuesday

Wednesday

Thursday

Friday

Saturday

Sunday

DOUG'S RULES FOR LIFE

Life can be complicated, but I've got it figured out

RULE 1:
Keep your friends
CLOSE

RULE 2:
And your snacks
CLOSER

RULE 3:
Stop to smell
(and taste)
the
FLOWERS

WHAT WOULD DOUG SAY?

can you tell what I'm thinking in these pics? Write down your best guess.

Happy Holipugs
WORD SEARCH

My favorite holiday things are hidden in this word search. Can you find them all?

```
K R Y O G O C G L A G T S N Y
K H W G S H V I K P N H E T I
U P Q W I A A N Q U Q A S K I
P I E L F P L G C G O N T I N
U Z A A S P E E O O Q K P U I
G Z S E P Y N R U L D S U J J
K A T V U H P P N A E P G D J
I T E K G O U U T N V U R S A
N R R T O L G G P T L G I I U
P E P I W I S H U E E G C Q B
I E U B E P D O G R C I K I Q
E F G Q E U A U U N R N S L E
L N G J N G Y S L X C G D F F
J X Y A O S Y E A U J Q A P G
Z M P R L R J M T P H P Y P X
```

See how you did on page 86!

52

DOUG's SELFIE TIPS

It takes an A++ selfie game to be Insta-famous. Here are some tips to make your selfies as good as mine.

SELFIE TIP #1
There's no such thing as a BAD ANGLE

When you've got no neck

The only time I had a flat tummy

When bees are chasing u

SELFIE TIP #2
Anything can be an
ACCESSORY

Flowers bring out your natural beauty

Tub style on point

Can u beleaf how cute I am?

Not sure about the burrito look

SELFIE TIP #3
Find a background as pretty as YOU ARE

SELFIE TIP #4
Dive in! Don't be afraid to
GO FOR IT.

59

SELFIE TIP #5
SMILE!

SELFIE TIP #6
Believe in Yourselfie

CAPTION MATCH

Can you match the picture to the caption? Draw a line to connect each photo with the caption you think fits best, then check your answers on page 86.

He sees you when you're sleeping

Rub a dub dub, pug in a tub

Do you think I ordered enough?

Hay girl

Happiness is a warm blanket

It's a Doug eat dog world

Snug as a pug in a rug

Hiding from the pugparazzi

Let sleeping Dougs lie

The four basic food groups

I love my fans

Is there something stuck in my teeth?

QUIZ: WHAT WOULD DOUG DO?

Now that you know me pretty well, what do you think I would do in the following situations?

1. Aliens are taking over the planet! WWDD?

a) Hide

b) Battle to save Earth

c) Put on a robe and order pizza

2. It's a cold and rainy day.

WWDD?

a) Stay in bed as long as possible

b) Warm up with some hot coffee

c) Put on rain gear and venture outside

d) All of the above

3. On the way to a big event your luggage gets lost.

WWDD?

a) Rush around and buy new clothes

b) Wear whatever is lying around

c) Who needs clothes when u have

PUGGITUDE!

4. Pugoween is coming!

WWDD?

a) Get a fancy store-bought costume

b) Throw something together at the last minute

c) What are you talking about? Every day is Pugoween!

5. Friends drop by unexpectedly while you're still in bed. WWDD?

a) Throw on a robe and invite them in

b) Get fully dressed before answering the door

c) Pretend you're not home

6. There's one piece of pizza left.

WWDD?

a) Save it for breakfast

b) Insist you take it

c) Offer to split it

d) Never mind, he ate it while you were reading this

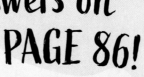
Check your answers on PAGE 86!

DOUG & ♥ FRIENDS

Sometimes on my pugventures I meet famous people. I try to be cool and not act pugstruck!

Me and the cast of Stranger Things

STARRING AS ELEVEN ON STRANGER PUGS

Half of my heart is with Camila Cabello

PUGVANA OOH NA-NA

Justin Bieber made a belieber out of me

Snuggle buddy, Joe Jonas

I'll be on Katy Perry's team any day

YouTubing with Miranda Sings

74

WHERE IN THE WORLD IS DOUG?

I love to travel! Can you tell where I am in these postcards? Make a guess, then draw in the background scenery. See where I am on page 87. Bon voyage!

GREETINGS from
The happiest place on Earth!

It's a Pug World after all!

BY AIR MAIL
PAR AVION

APPROVED
12345

AIR MAIL

BONJOUR!

76

ARRIVAL
12345

Greetings from Jolly Olde

WISH YOU WERE HERE!

I ♥ NY

ARRIVAL
45

78

Greetings *from the* Sunshine State!

QUIZ: How well do you know DOUG?

Test your D.Q. (Doug Quotient) with this fun quiz!

1. Where do I live?
   a) Los Angeles, California
   b) Boston, Massachusetts
   c) Nashville, Tennessee
   d) Dallas, Texas

2. Who is my sibling?
   a) Frank the parrot
   b) Winston the hamster
   c) Todd the fish
   d) Fiona the cat

3. What is my favorite season?
   a) Summer
   b) Spring
   c) Fall
   d) Winter

4. My wardrobe essentials:
   a) Suit & tie
   b) Tutu, leather jacket, boa
   c) Beanie, robe, shades
   d) Onesie, baseball cap, slippers

5. What's my favorite thing to eat?
   a) Salad
   b) Pizza
   c) Tacos
   d) Grilled cheese

6. When did I begin posting on Instagram?
   a) 2015
   b) 2018
   c) 2012
   d) 1999

7. Who are my parents?
   a) Leslie & Rob
   b) Leslie & Fiona
   c) Fiona & Rob
   d) Melissa & Elijah

8. I am known as
   a) Sir Douglas of Puggington
   b) Doug, Prince of Pugs
   c) King of Pop Culture
   d) Lord Dougington of Pugsly Square

GET YOUR SCORE ON PAGE 87!

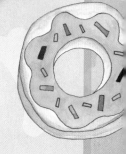

DOUG's
RECIPE for SUCCESS

Recipe

Three cups
hard work

UNITED STATES
POSTAL SERVICE

Recipe

Four cups coffee

Recipe

2 teaspoons
pure
PUGGITUDE

Recipe

Sprinkle with puggeroni

Recipe

Bake for ten minutes

Recipe

Serve with love! (And sprinkles!)

ANSWER KEY

From page 52: Word Search

From page 62: Caption Match

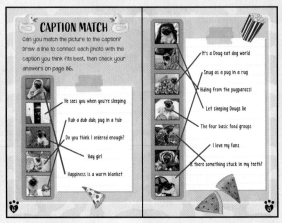

From page 65: Quiz — What Would Doug Do?

1. C — Put on a robe and order pizza
2. D — All of the above
3. C — Who needs clothes when u have PUGGITUDE!
4. C — What are you talking about? Every day is Pugoween!
5. A — Throw on a robe and invite them in
6. D — Never mind, he ate it while you were reading this

SCORING:

Give yourself 1 point for every question answered correctly.

IF YOU HAVE:

5-6 Points — Two Pugs in a Pod!

Have you looked in the mirror lately because I'm pretty sure you're a pug, too.

3-4 Points — Not a pug.

Maybe a golden retriever.

1-2 Points — Definitely not a pug.

You are obviously a human.

From page 75: Where in the World is Doug?

Disney World, Florida

Paris, France

London, England

New York City, New York

Orlando, Florida

From page 80: Quiz — How Well Do You Know Doug?

1. C — Nashville, Tennessee
2. D — Fiona the cat
3. C — Fall
4. C — Beanie, robe, shades
5. B — Pizza
6. A — 2015
7. A — Leslie & Rob
8. C — King of Pop Culture

SCORING:

Give yourself 1 point for every correct answer.

IF YOU HAVE:

1-3 points — LOW D.Q.

Did you even read this book? You should read it again. Return to page 1.

4-6 points — AVERAGE D.Q.

You can do better! Raise your D.Q. by reading this book at least three more times.

7-8 points — HIGH D.Q.

You are Doug's biggest fan! Turn to page 15 to see how Doug feels about you.

Thanks for hanging out with me! It was fun getting to know each other.

I hope you never leave home without your puggitude and you'll never forget to bring style, spirit, adventure, and pizza to your life! —XO **DOUG**

Wanna hang out some more? Turn the page for your very own Doug the Pug!

P.S. I'm pretty laid-back, but not all dogs (or cats, or any other animals!) are created the same. I wouldn't recommend dressing up your pets or anyone else's, or giving them any of my favorite foods—they may not like it!

DRESS DOUG!

Want to take selfies and eat pizza together? Cut out the images of me and my accessories on pages 93 and 95 and glue them on heavier paper or an old greeting card! When dry, cut out the adorable picture of me, the stand, clothes, and accessories. Now you can dress me up for every season and mood!

Foldline

Tab

Ask an adult for help. Cut Doug out along the dotted lines. To make Doug stand, fold the white part of the base back. On the next page, cut out the support along the lines. Fold at the foldline indicated to form a tab. Center the tab on Doug's back with the lower edge even with the fold in the base. Tape or glue in place. For the accessories, carefully cut along the dotted lines and use the tabs to place the accessories on Doug. Use tape to secure the tabs, if needed.

91

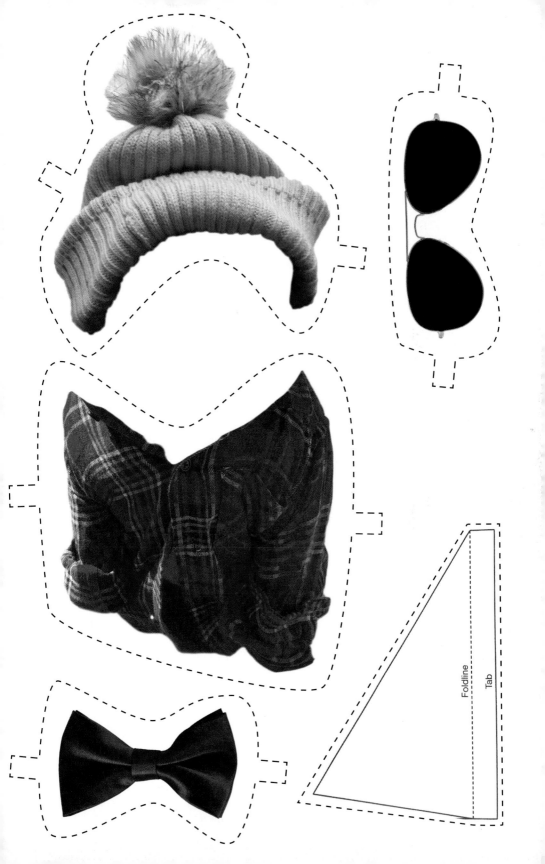

Foldline

Tab

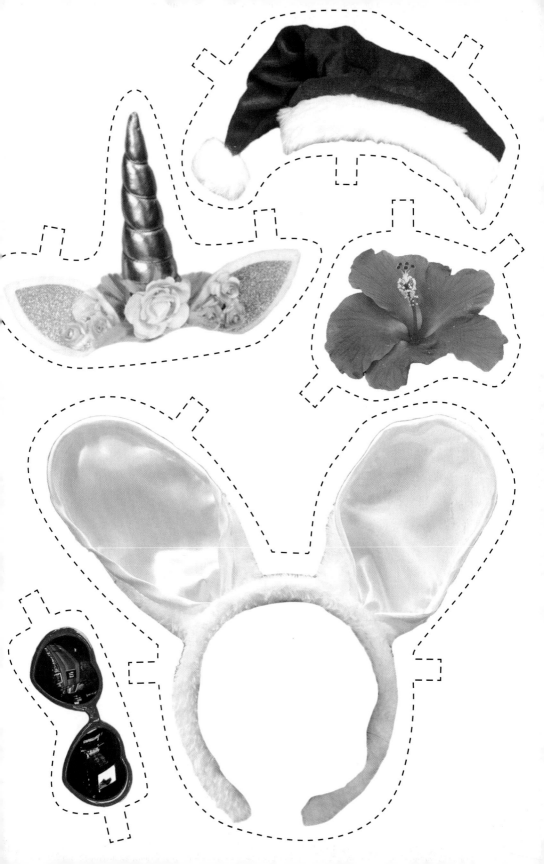